Contents Guide

Section 1: Introduction

1. Welcome & What You'll Learn
2. World of APIs: An Overview

Section 2: Demystifying APIs and RESTful APIs

3. Decoding APIs: A Simplified Perspective
4. Navigating Real-Life Scenarios with APIs
5. Exploring Language Flexibility in API Integration
6. Introduction to the Art of RESTful APIs
7. Unveiling the Power of JSON
8. Realizing Concepts with a Practical JavaScript API Example
9. Engaging with GET Requests: Unearthing Data
10. Mastering the Art of POST Requests: Sending Data
11. Deleting Data: Understanding DELETE Requests
12. Updating Data: The Power of PUT/PATCH Requests
13. Embracing API Consumption: A User's Guide
14. Dialogue Between Requests and Responses
15. Deciphering the Language of Status Codes
16. Safeguarding Your APIs: The Realm of API Security

Section 3: Mastering API Integration

17. Best Practices for API Documentation: Crafting Clear Guidelines
18. Versioning APIs: Managing Changes Seamlessly
19. Performance Optimization Techniques: Maximizing Efficiency
20. Error Handling Strategies: Navigating Through Challenges
21. API Testing Essentials: Ensuring Reliability
22. Monitoring and Analytics: Keeping a Pulse on Your APIs
23. Scalability Considerations: Preparing for Growth
24. Future Trends in Web Communication: Embracing Innovations

→ *REST API Cheat Sheet*
→ *Conclusion*

Section 1: Introduction

Welcome & What You'll Learn

Welcome to the exciting world of APIs and the power they wield in shaping modern web communication! This book is your gateway to understanding the core concepts driving how countless applications, websites, and services interact behind the scenes.

The API Revolution

Think of websites or apps you use every day – weather forecasts, social media, online shopping - they all rely on APIs. Imagine APIs as invisible messengers. They allow different software systems to share information and perform tasks without you having to navigate the complexities of each one individually.

Why Mastering APIs Matters (Even If You Don't Code)

You don't have to be a programmer to benefit immensely from understanding APIs. Whether you're a:

- **Business Owner:** Explore ways to streamline operations and unlock new growth opportunities by integrating apps and services.
- **Product Manager:** Discover how APIs can enhance your product offerings and create seamless user experiences.
- **Marketer:** Understand how APIs power data-driven marketing strategies and customer insights.
- **Technologist:** Learn how to integrate various systems within your company or for clients.
- **Curious Individual:** Demystify how the digital world functions, fostering a deeper understanding of the technology you interact with daily.

What You Will Learn

This book unfolds the world of APIs in a clear and concise way, starting with the fundamentals and progressing to more advanced concepts. You'll learn:

- **The Core Mechanics of APIs:** How they work and the language they use for communication.
- **RESTful API Principles:** Delve into the most popular architectural style for building APIs.
- **API Requests and Responses:** Master how to retrieve data, submit information, update, and delete resources.
- **Consuming APIs for Real-World Use Cases:** Explore practical examples across various industries.
- **API Security, Optimization, and Testing:** Ensure your APIs are safe, efficient, and reliable.
- **Future of APIs:** Discover the cutting-edge trends shaping the API landscape.

Getting the Most Out of This Book

You'll gain the most from this book by actively experimenting as you learn. Many websites offer free APIs, so you can test the principles we discuss. Here's a simple example to get you started:

1. **Visit the OpenWeatherMap website:** (https://openweathermap.org/)
2. **Sign up for a free API key.**
3. **Experiment with their API to fetch real-time weather data for your city.**

By the end of this book, you'll have a solid grasp of this technology, the power it holds, and how you can harness it strategically.

Let's Embark on This Learning Adventure!

Additional Resources:

- **Mozilla Developer Network (MDN) Intro to APIs:**
  https://developer.mozilla.org/en-US/docs/Web/API
- **"What is an API?" from DigitalOcean:**
  https://www.digitalocean.com/community/tutorials/what-is-an-api

World of APIs: An Overview

In the previous chapter, we ignited your curiosity about APIs. Now, let's go on a journey to explore their vast ecosystem and the exciting ways they shape how applications interact with each other in the digital realm.

APIs: The Hidden Fabric of the Web

Think of the internet as a bustling digital metropolis. Websites are the storefronts, apps are specialized services, and APIs are the intricate network of roads and pathways that connect everything together. Let's explore some common scenarios:

- **Booking a Trip:** When you book a flight or hotel online, the travel site likely uses APIs to communicate with airline reservation systems, hotel availability databases, and even map services.
- **Social Media Magic:** Sharing an article on social media triggers APIs that allow your social network to fetch a preview, including the title and image, directly from the article's website.
- **Smart Devices:** Your smart thermostat adjusting the temperature based on weather forecasts? APIs are making that communication possible.

Types of APIs

The world of APIs is diverse. Here's a glimpse into some common categories:

- **Open APIs (Public APIs):** These are freely available for developers to use, often provided by large tech companies like Google Maps, Twitter, and many more.
- **Partner APIs:** Designed for collaboration between specific businesses with established partnerships. They aid in streamlined integration between the partners' systems.
- **Internal APIs (Private APIs):** Used within an organization to connect different departments and systems. They help to improve internal communication and efficiency.

APIs for All Industries

APIs are not limited to just technology companies! Their impact spans various sectors:

- **Finance:** APIs power secure online transactions, real-time stock updates, and integration with accounting software.
- **Healthcare:** APIs enable the exchange of patient data, appointment scheduling, and the integration of medical devices for monitoring.
- **E-commerce:** Smooth product searches, inventory management, payment processing, and shipping integration are all driven by APIs.
- **Government:** APIs are transforming how government services work, making data more accessible, and allowing for the creation of more efficient citizen-facing applications.

The Benefits: Why APIs Matter

- **Enhanced Efficiency:** APIs automate tasks, saving time and effort for both businesses and users.
- **Innovation:** APIs enable new services and features by combining the capabilities of existing systems.
- **Data-Driven Insights:** APIs make it easier to gather and analyze data from multiple sources, helping businesses make better decisions.
- **Collaboration:** APIs foster integration across teams, companies, and even industries.

The Next Step in Your Journey

Understanding the world of APIs has set the foundation for your deeper exploration. In the following chapters, we'll start breaking down the technical aspects of how APIs work, their language, and how you can harness their power.

Additional Resources

- **ProgrammableWeb API Directory:** https://www.programmableweb.com/apis/directory (Explore a massive collection of APIs across various categories)
- **Postman: An API Exploration Tool:** https://www.postman.com/ (Experiment with interacting with APIs directly)

Section 2:
Demystifying APIs and RESTful APIs

Decoding APIs: A Simplified Perspective

APIs might sound mysterious and technical, but in this chapter, we'll demystify them! We'll shed the jargon and reveal the straightforward concepts that drive API communication.

Think of APIs as Restaurants

Imagine a restaurant. You, the customer, don't need to know all the complexities happening in the kitchen to enjoy your meal. Here's how this relates to APIs:

- **The Menu (API Documentation):** The menu lists what you can order. Similarly, API documentation tells developers what data they can access and what actions they can perform with the API.
- **Placing Your Order (API Request):** You choose a dish from the menu and tell the waiter. This is like sending an API request – you're stating what you want.
- **The Kitchen's Work (API Processing):** The kitchen prepares your food based on your order. The API processes your request, going into its system to find the data or carry out the task you requested.
- **Food Served! (API Response):** The waiter brings your meal. That's the API response - data or confirmation of your completed action.

The Magic of API Requests

Let's imagine you want the current weather in your city. Here's how an API would help:

1. **Finding the Right 'Restaurant':** You find a weather API (like OpenWeatherMap).
2. **Reading the 'Menu':** The API documentation tells you how to request weather data for a specific location.
3. **Making the Order':** You send an API request with your city's name.

4. **The 'Kitchen' Does Its Work:** The weather API checks its vast database of current weather information.
5. **Your 'Meal' Is Delivered:** The API sends back a response with the temperature, conditions (sunny, rainy, etc.), and other details.

The Secret Ingredient: URLs

In the digital world, API requests are made using special web addresses called URLs. Here's a simplified example:

https://api.weathersite.com/current?city=London

- `https://api.weathersite.com/current`: This part identifies the weather API we're communicating with.
- `?city=London`: This is where we specify the information needed for our request (to get the weather in London).

Beyond the Basics

Of course, APIs can be more complex than a restaurant analogy. They may require special 'keys' (for security) and use different ways to format data. Don't worry, we'll tackle these concepts gradually. For now, focus on the core idea of sending requests and getting responses.

Additional Resources

- **"Explain Like I'm Five (ELI5): What is an API?":** https://www.reddit.com/r/explainlikeimfive/comments/nb7ilg/eli5_what_is_an_api/ (Find real-world explanations of APIs in plain language)
- **API Basics Tutorial:** https://developer.mozilla.org/en-US/docs/Learn/JavaScript/Client-side_web_APIs/Introduction (Provides a beginner-friendly overview)

Get Ready to Dive Deeper!

Now that you understand the essence of APIs, we're ready to explore real-life examples and discover the power of this versatile technology.

Navigating Real-Life Scenarios with APIs

We've grasped the basic workings of APIs; now let's visualize how they seamlessly integrate into our daily lives and the solutions they power. Get ready to discover how APIs transform the way we interact with technology!

Scenario 1: The Magic of Social Media

- **Sharing News Across Platforms:** Clicking "share" on a news article and instantly posting it on Twitter? APIs connect the news site and your social network.
- **Friend Suggestions:** Ever wondered how Facebook suggests "People You May Know"? It leverages APIs to analyze your network, shared interests, location data, and more.
- **Live Video or Chat Integration:** Apps embedding live video streaming or chat features within their platforms often use APIs offered by specialized services.

Scenario 2: Travel Planning Made Easy

- **Comparing Flights and Hotels:** A website comparing prices across numerous airlines and hotels isn't manually checking each one. It uses travel APIs!
- **Real-Time Updates:** Receiving timely notifications about flight delays or gate changes? APIs maintain the constant flow of information.
- **Map Integrations:** When booking a trip, those interactive maps displaying hotels and attractions in your destination city are powered by map APIs (like Google Maps).

Scenario 3: The Power of Online Shopping

- **Smooth Payment Experiences:** Secure payment gateways like PayPal or Stripe utilize APIs to process transactions, reducing friction for both shoppers and merchants.
- **Shipping Options:** When you're offered different shipping choices and rates at checkout, your e-commerce store is communicating with shipping carrier APIs.
- **Real-Time Inventory Tracking:** That "In Stock" or "Only 2 Left!" message you see reflects APIs updating inventory levels in real-time.

Scenario 4: Smart Homes and IoT

- **Voice Control:** "Alexa, turn on the lights!" Voice assistants interact with smart devices through APIs, relaying your commands and retrieving information.
- **Remote Monitoring:** Checking your home security camera feed while away, or adjusting your thermostat from your phone? APIs make it possible.
- **Connecting Disparate Devices:** APIs ensure your smart coffee maker, fitness tracker, and light bulbs can 'talk' to each other or work with automation platforms.

Beyond the Obvious

APIs are working behind the scenes in countless other ways:

- **Customer Relationship Management (CRM) Tools:** APIs help track sales leads, customer interactions, and more.
- **Marketing Automation:** APIs power syncing email campaigns, targeted social media ads, and personalized recommendations.
- **Government Data Portals:** Open government APIs provide access to valuable data sets on demographics, healthcare, and more.

The Takeaway

The vast number of APIs demonstrates how deeply they're woven into the modern digital experience. Understanding their capabilities opens up a world of possibilities for streamlining tasks, connecting services, and unlocking new innovations.

Additional Resources

- **"Ways APIs are Used in Everyday Life" Article:** https://nordicapis.com/5-examples-of-apis-we-use-in-our-everyday-lives/
- **Interesting API Use Cases:** https://www.programmableweb.com/news/20-interesting-use-cases-for-apis/analysis/2019/02/14 (Explore diverse APIs on ProgrammableWeb's directory)

Let's continue exploring how APIs utilize specific languages and structures for seamless communication!

Exploring Language Flexibility in API Integration

One of the greatest strengths of APIs is their remarkable language adaptability. Think of this as their ability to 'speak' the language of the systems they're connecting. Just as you might talk to someone in English, Spanish, or another language, APIs can tailor their data exchange to match the programming environment they're working within.

How APIs Achieve Language Flexibility

- **Data Formats:** APIs commonly use data formats like JSON (which we'll cover) and XML. These formats provide structured ways to package information that can be understood by computers, regardless of the specific programming language.
- **Libraries and Tools:** Many programming languages have libraries and tools designed specifically to interact with APIs. These tools handle the "translation" work, enabling seamless data exchange.
- **Language-Neutral Design:** Well-designed APIs often aim to be as language-neutral as possible, making them simpler to integrate with a diverse range of systems.

Let's See It in Action

Imagine a shipping company with an API that lets its business clients fetch shipping rates. Here's how the API's language flexibility comes into play:

- **Client A's System (Python):** Client A's website is built using Python. Their developers use Python libraries to send requests to the shipping API and receive the rates in a way their Python code understands.
- **Client B's System (Java):** Client B has an accounting system written in Java. Using Java tools for working with APIs, they fetch the same shipping rate information in a format compatible with their software.

Though both clients use different technologies, the API can serve them both!

Real-World Examples

- **Cloud Services:** Cloud providers like Amazon Web Services (AWS), Microsoft Azure, and Google Cloud offer extensive APIs. Developers

building applications with a variety of programming languages can use these APIs to control cloud storage, databases, and more.
- **E-commerce APIs:** Platforms like Shopify and BigCommerce provide APIs that allow developers to integrate their online stores with inventory management systems, accounting tools, or even custom-built applications, regardless of the technology involved.
- **Mapping APIs:** Google Maps APIs can be integrated into websites and apps built with different languages, enabling developers to add interactive maps, get directions, and utilize location data.

Why Language Flexibility Matters

- **Reduced Barriers:** Language flexibility breaks down silos between different software systems, allowing seamless connections regardless of how each individual system is built.
- **Innovation:** It fosters innovation by allowing developers to combine the strengths of diverse tools and technologies.
- **Freedom of Choice:** Businesses and individuals aren't locked into specific technology stacks. They can choose the best programming languages and tools for the task at hand.

Additional Resources

- **Intro to Web APIs from Web.dev:** https://web.dev/web-apis/ (Provides a general overview of API concepts)

Introduction to the Art of RESTful APIs

Up until now, we've explored the world of APIs in a broader sense. Now, it's time to focus on the most widely adopted approach to designing APIs: REST (Representational State Transfer). Let's unravel what makes RESTful APIs so popular and how they create a well-organized foundation for web communication.

What Does REST Mean?

REST is not a technology itself; it's an architectural style, a set of guidelines that shape how an API should be designed. At its core, REST emphasizes:

- **Resources:** Everything in a RESTful API revolves around resources, which can be any piece of information like weather data, a product in a store, a customer profile, etc. Each resource is identified by a unique address (URL).
- **Representations:** Resources can be represented in different formats (like JSON or XML), enabling flexibility.
- **Statelessness:** In RESTful APIs, each API request is self-contained with all the information needed for the server to process it. The server doesn't maintain 'sessions' or remember previous requests from the same client.
- **Uniform Interface:** REST defines a specific set of actions (which we'll explore), fostering consistency.

The Benefits of Being RESTful

- **Widely Adopted**: Due to REST's popularity, you'll find countless tools, libraries, and tutorials supporting it, easing integration for developers in any technology.
- **Scalability:** Statelessness makes RESTful APIs scalable – they can easily handle a growing number of requests.
- **Cacheability:** REST often enables caching for improved performance, storing responses to reduce the server load for repeated requests.
- **Intuitive:** REST APIs frequently follow logical, human-readable patterns, making them easier to learn and use.

How RESTful APIs Map to Real-World Concepts

Think of a RESTful API as a well-organized library:

- **Books Are Resources:** Each book (on history, science fiction, etc.) is a resource with its unique identifier.
- **Representations:** You can get information about a book in different formats (physical copy, e-book, audiobook).
- **Stateless Librarian:** The librarian doesn't remember your previous searches. You provide information about the book you need each time.
- **Uniform Actions:** You have a standard set of actions: borrow, return, renew, search the catalog.

REST in Action

Imagine a RESTful API for movie information:

- **GET /movies/12345** - Fetches details of the movie with ID 12345
- **POST /movies** - Adds a new movie to the database.
- **DELETE /movies/12345** - Deletes the movie with ID 12345.

Notice the clear pattern using URLs for resources and standard actions.

Additional Resources

- **REST API Tutorial:** https://restfulapi.net/
- **"What is REST" from IBM Cloud:** https://www.ibm.com/cloud/learn/rest-apis

Next Up: Mastering JSON

RESTful APIs often rely on a specific data format called JSON for exchanging data. Let's unveil the power of JSON in the next chapter!

Unveiling the Power of JSON

Meet JSON (JavaScript Object Notation), a simple yet incredibly versatile way to structure data. Imagine JSON as a universal translator, helping different systems understand each other by providing a common language for information exchange. Let's explore its structure and the reasons why it's so beloved for use with APIs.

The Foundations of JSON

JSON uses a straightforward format of key-value pairs and easily recognizable structures:

- **Key-Value Pairs:** A key is like a label (wrapped in double quotes), followed by a colon, and then its associated value. Example: `"city": "London"`
- **Objects:** A collection of key-value pairs enclosed in curly braces `{ }`. Example: `{ "city": "London", "temperature": 20, "conditions": "Sunny" }`
- **Arrays:** An ordered list of values enclosed in square brackets `[ ]`. Arrays can contain numbers, strings, objects, or even other arrays. Example: `[ "apple", "banana", "orange" ]`

Example: Let's Imagine a Book in JSON

```
{
   "title": "APIs Explained",
   "author": "Your Name",
   "year": 2024,
   "chapters": [ "Introduction", "REST Basics", "Advanced Concepts" ]
}
```

Why JSON is Ideal for APIs

- **Human-Readable:** JSON's syntax is easy for both humans and computers to understand, promoting clarity.
- **Lightweight:** JSON minimizes overhead, making data transmission between systems fast and efficient.

- **Language-Neutral:** As we touched on in the previous chapter, JSON can be easily processed by any programming language, fostering compatibility.
- **Hierarchical Structures:** JSON's support for nested data (objects within objects, arrays of objects) allows for representing complex information.

JSON in the Real World

Let's see how a weather API might respond with JSON data:

```
{
    "city": "Los Angeles",
    "current_temp": 25,
    "conditions": "Sunny",
    "forecast": [
        { "day": "Monday", "high": 28 },
        { "day": "Tuesday", "high": 26 }
    ]
}
```

Notice how the JSON structure mirrors real-world concepts, making the data easy to interpret.

JSON in Action

Most modern web browsers let you directly view JSON returned by APIs. Experiment with this yourself:

1. Visit the Open Weather API: https://openweathermap.org/
2. Sign up for a free API Key.
3. Make a test API request in your browser for a city. The response you'll see is JSON!

Additional Resources

- **JSON Introduction:** https://www.w3schools.com/js/js_json_intro.asp
- **Learn JSON:** https://www.json.org/
- **JSON Validator:** https://jsonlint.com/ (Useful for checking if JSON data is well-formatted)

Next: Making Sense of API Requests

Now that you understand the core way APIs represent data, we're ready to explore how API requests are structured and the methods used to fetch and manipulate information.

Realizing Concepts with a Practical JavaScript API Example

It's time to move from theory to practice. In this chapter, we'll roll up our sleeves and interact with a live API using JavaScript. Our goal is to fetch some exciting data and make it tangible, providing you with a clear understanding of how API integration actually works.

Our Mission: Exploring Quotes

We'll be using the 'They Said So' API, which provides a vast collection of inspirational quotes. Here's what we'll do:

1. Fetch a random quote
2. Display the quote and its author on a simple webpage.

Prerequisites

- **Basic HTML Knowledge:** You should understand the structure of a simple HTML file with `<div>` elements to hold content.
- **Understanding of JavaScript Variables:** Knowing how to create variables in JavaScript will be helpful.

Step 1 - The API Playground

First, let's explore the API directly.

1. Visit the 'They Said So' documentation: [invalid URL removed]
2. Note how the API lets you fetch random or categorized quotes. We'll focus on the random quote generation.

Step 2 - Simple HTML Setup

Create an HTML file (name it `index.html`) with the following:

```
<!DOCTYPE html>
<html>
<head>
   <title>Quote Fetcher</title>
</head>
<body>
   <div id="quote-content"></div>
```

```
  <div id="quote-author"></div>
  <script>
    // Our JavaScript code will go here
  </script>
 </body>
</html>
```

Step 3 - The JavaScript Magic

Inside the `<script>` tags, paste the following code. Don't worry, we'll break it down!

```
fetch('https://api.theysaidso.com/qod')
    .then(response => response.json()) // Convert response to JSON
    .then(data => {

document.getElementById('quote-content').textContent = data.contents.quotes[0].quote;

document.getElementById('quote-author').textContent = "- " + data.contents.quotes[0].author;
    })
    .catch(error => console.error('Error fetching:', error)); // Error Handling
```

Explanation

- **fetch():** This is the star that kickstarts fetching data from the API. We provide the API URL as input.
- **then() Chains:** Think of each `.then()` as a step in processing the API response, converting it into usable JSON, and finally updating elements on your web page.
- **Error Handling:** The `.catch()` ensures we're gracefully handling any issues that might arise during the API call.

Open Your HTML File in a Browser

A random quote should appear on your simple webpage! Refresh the page for a new one.

Additional Resources

- **Introduction to `fetch()`:**
  https://developer.mozilla.org/en-US/docs/Web/API/Fetch_API/Using_Fetch
- **Theysaidso API Documentation:** https://theysaidso.com/api/

Let's Continue Exploring!

This was just a taste of API interactions using JavaScript. Next, we'll dive into the specific types of API requests (GET, POST, and more) used for different tasks.

Engaging with GET Requests: Unearthing Data

In the realm of APIs, GET requests are like your trusty detectives. Their primary mission is to fetch data from a specific resource. Imagine you want weather information, product details, the latest news headlines – this is where GET requests step in.

The Anatomy of a GET Request

At their core, GET requests are remarkably straightforward:

- **The URL (The Address):** This is the unique address of the resource you want to access, much like a house address. For example: `https://api.openweathermap.org/data/2.5/weather?city=Berlin`
- **Parameters (Optional Instructions):** These are additional pieces of information that refine your request. Think of them as specific instructions for your detective. In our example, `?city=Berlin` provides the city name.

Real-World Examples with GET

- **Searching for Books by Title:** A library catalog API might use a GET request like: `https://library-api.org/books?title=Dune`
- **Fetching Social Media Posts:** A social media API might let you retrieve a user's latest posts with a GET request to: `https://socialnetwork.com/posts/username`
- **Checking Order Status:** An e-commerce API could have a GET request with an order ID to fetch order details: `https://store.com/orders/12345`

Under the Hood of GET

1. **Your Web Browser is Key:** Often, you interact with GET requests behind the scenes when you click a link, enter a search term, or load a website! Your browser assembles the GET request and sends it to the relevant API.

2. **The Server Responds:** The API server receives the GET request, processes it, gathers the needed data, and packages it into a response (commonly using JSON).
3. **Data Displayed:** Your browser interprets the response and updates the webpage to display the information for you.

Why GET Requests Are So Popular

- **Retrieving Data Only:** GET requests are designed for fetching, not modifying data. This makes them simple and safe (you won't accidentally change something).
- **Cache-Friendly:** Responses to GET requests can often be cached by browsers or by systems in between. This speeds up repeat requests for the same resource.
- **Bookmarkable:** Because GET request parameters are reflected in the URL, you can bookmark or share links that represent specific searches or data views.

Experimenting with GET Requests

The easiest way to experience GET requests is directly in your web browser! Here's a safe API to experiment with:

- **JSONPlaceholder (Fake Data for Testing):** https://jsonplaceholder.typicode.com/
- Try accessing:
    - `https://jsonplaceholder.typicode.com/posts` (to get a list of blog posts)
    - `https://jsonplaceholder.typicode.com/posts/1` (to get details of post with ID 1)

Additional Resources

- **HTTP GET Method Explained:** https://www.w3schools.com/tags/ref_httpmethods.asp
- **Visualizing HTTP Requests:** https://httptoolkit.tech/ (A tool to view and intercept API requests)

Next Up: The Power of Sending Data

GET requests excel at fetching information, but what if you need to send new data to a server? That's where POST requests come into play, which we'll cover in the next chapter.

Mastering the Art of POST Requests: Sending Data

While GET requests are about retrieving data, POST requests are focused on sending data to a server to create or update resources. Think of POST requests as the delivery service for your API interactions. Let's see them in action!

When POST Requests Take the Stage

- **Submitting Forms:** When you fill out a contact form, sign up for an account, or place an online order, chances are a POST request is working behind the scenes to transmit your information.
- **Creating Social Media Posts:** Adding a new post on your favorite social media platform likely involves a POST request to create that post on their servers.
- **Uploading Files:** Attaching a resume to a job application or uploading a photo to an image-sharing website often relies on POST requests to handle the file transfer.
- **API-Driven Data Input:** Applications that allow users to add custom data (like notes, to-do list items, etc.) frequently use POST requests to store new entries.

Anatomy of a POST Request

- **The URL:** Like GET requests, POST requests target a specific URL representing the resource location where you want to send the data.
- ****The Request Body: **** This is the **key difference** from GET. POST requests carry the data to be sent within their body, packaged in a format like JSON or form data.

POST Request in the Wild

Let's imagine a blog commenting API:

- **URL:** `https://blogapi.com/comments`
- **POST Body (JSON format):**

```
{

  "postId": 5,
```

```
    "author": "Alice",
    "content": "Great article!"
}
```

How POST Works Under the Surface

1. **Data Packaging:** Your browser or application assembles the POST request, including the URL and the data to be sent in the body.
2. **Server Receives and Processes:** The API server receives your POST request, unpacks the data, and performs the relevant actions (like storing your comment in a database).
3. **Response:** The server sends back a response, usually confirming the success of the operation or providing details about the newly created resource.

Why Use POST

- **Sending New Information:** POST requests are designed for creating new entries or resources on the server.
- **Flexibility in Data Sent:** You can submit substantial or complex data using formats like JSON.
- **No Direct Exposure in the URL:** Unlike GET requests, sensitive data isn't included as visible parameters in the URL, offering a layer of security.

Not Just Browsers: Using POST Requests

Web browsers play a crucial role in everyday POST interactions, but you can also use tools and libraries. Here are a few:

- **API Testing Tools:** Tools like Postman (https://www.postman.com/) allow you to experiment with POST requests directly.
- **Programming Languages:** All programming languages have ways to send POST requests when building applications.

Additional Resources

- **HTTP POST Method Explained:**
  https://www.w3schools.com/tags/ref_httpmethods.asp

- **Working with POST Requests in JavaScript:**
  https://developer.mozilla.org/en-US/docs/Web/API/Fetch_API/Using_Fetch

Next Up: Deleting with DELETE Requests

Now that you understand how to retrieve (GET) and send (POST) data with APIs, the next logical step is exploring ways to delete resources with the DELETE request method.

Deleting Data: Understanding DELETE Requests

In the world of RESTful APIs, DELETE requests hold the power of removal. Their purpose is straightforward: to delete a specific resource identified by its URL.

When DELETE Requests Come Into Play

- **Removing Blog Comments:** A blog API might allow you to delete your own comments using a DELETE request.
- **E-commerce Order Cancellation:** Deleting an order you placed on an e-commerce site could involve a DELETE request.
- **Social Media Cleanup:** APIs often let you delete old posts or other content using DELETE.
- **Managing Data in Applications:** Applications with custom data-editing features might use DELETE requests to erase items like notes or tasks.

The Essence of a DELETE Request

- **The Target URL:** Like other API requests, the URL specifies the exact resource you want to delete. Example: `https://api.todolist.com/tasks/27` to delete task with ID 27.

The Simple Process

1. **Request Sent:** Your application or browser sends a DELETE request to the specified URL.
2. **Authorization Checks:** The API often verifies if you have permission to delete the resource.
3. **Deletion:** If authorized, the server removes the resource from its system.
4. **Confirmation:** Typically, the server sends a response confirming the deletion or an error message if something goes wrong.

Why DELETE is Special

- **Designed for Removal:** DELETE has the singular purpose of deleting resources.

- **Idempotence:** A fancy term meaning you can send the same DELETE request multiple times, and the result will be the same – the resource will be deleted (or stay deleted).

DELETE in Your Browser (with Caution!)

Most of the time, you'll indirectly trigger DELETE requests through buttons or links within a website or application. However, for experimentation, some API testing tools allow you to send DELETE requests manually. **Use this power with great caution!**

A Word of Warning

- **Irreversible (Often):** In many cases, deletions triggered by DELETE requests are permanent. Double-check before making requests!
- **Authorization Matters:** APIs implement safeguards to ensure only authorized users or applications can delete resources.

Additional Resources

- **HTTP DELETE Method Explained:**
  https://www.w3schools.com/tags/ref_httpmethods.asp

Let's Move on to Updates: PUT/PATCH

Now that you understand how to remove data with DELETE, let's explore how APIs handle modifying existing resources using the PUT and PATCH requests.

Updating Data: The Power of PUT/PATCH Requests

GET brings data, POST creates new resources, DELETE removes them... but what if you need to change existing information? Enter the dynamic duo of PUT and PATCH requests, designed specifically for updating data on a server.

PUT vs. PATCH: Key Differences

- **PUT: Full Replacement:** PUT requests generally replace the entire resource at the target URL with the data you provide in the request body. Think of it like overwriting an existing file.
- **PATCH: Partial Updates:** PATCH requests are for modifying specific parts of a resource. You only send the fields you want to change. It's like carefully editing specific sections of a document.

When to Use Each

- **PUT:** * You have the complete updated representation of a resource. * You need to ensure the server's version perfectly matches what you send.
- **PATCH:** * Changing only a few fields within a larger resource. * Optimizing to send less data and reduce bandwidth usage.

Real-World Scenarios

Let's imagine an API for managing a user's profile:

- **PUT** `https://api.yourapp.com/profile`
    - Used to update an entire profile (username, email, address, etc.).
- **PATCH** `https://api.yourapp.com/profile`
    - Used to change just the user's email address or username.

PUT and PATCH in Action

Example: PUT request (full replacement)

PUT https://api.blog.com/posts/5
Body (JSON format):
{
　"title": "My Updated Article",
　"author": "Alice",

```
  "content": "Here's the revised content...",
  "publishedDate": "2024-03-18"
}
```

Example: PATCH request (partial update)

```
PATCH https://api.blog.com/posts/5
Body (JSON format):
{
   "title": "My Updated Article Title"
}
```

The Power of Choice

REST doesn't mandate that you must support both PUT and PATCH. An API could implement only one or the other, depending on its use cases.

Additional Resources

- **HTTP PUT Method:** https://www.w3schools.com/tags/ref_httpmethods.asp
- **HTTP PATCH Method:** https://www.rfc-editor.org/rfc/rfc5789.html

Next: Using APIs from a User's Perspective

So far, we've focused on the mechanics of API requests. Next, let's shift gears and explore how everyday users and applications interact with APIs, often without even realizing it!

Embracing API Consumption: A User's Guide

You might be surprised how deeply woven APIs are into your digital experiences, often working invisibly behind the scenes. Think of APIs as the hidden bridges that fuel the functionality of the tools you rely on.

APIs in Your Daily Life (Without You Knowing!)

- **Browsing Social Media:** Scrolling through posts, liking content, and sharing updates all involve numerous API calls happening behind the scenes.
- **Online Shopping:** Adding items to a cart, comparing products from different stores, and completing checkout processes often rely heavily on APIs.
- **Travel Planning:** When you search for the best flight deals across various websites, travel aggregators use APIs to compare prices from different airlines in real-time.
- **Getting Directions:** Mapping apps retrieve accurate and updated map data, traffic conditions, and route suggestions via APIs.
- **Smart Devices and IoT:** Sending commands to your smart lights, thermostat, or robot vacuum cleaner likely involves their associated APIs.

How Users Benefit from APIs

- **Connected Experiences:** Apps and websites can offer features that pull data from or interact with other platforms, creating a more streamlined experience.
- **Real-time Updates:** APIs power up-to-the-minute information, whether it's news, stock prices, or live sports scores.
- **Data Mashups:** APIs enable innovative services that aggregate data from various sources, offering new insights and value.

APIs for Businesses

API consumption isn't just for individual users. Businesses leverage APIs for:

- **Integrating with Partners:** APIs streamline data flow between a company and its suppliers, partners, or affiliates.

- **Extending their Services:** Businesses can open up their data or functionality via APIs to allow for external innovation and new applications.
- **Internal Systems:** Modern companies often use APIs to connect different software systems or platforms within their organization.

Indirect API Interaction

The beauty is, for most users, you don't need to know any coding or the intricacies of API requests:

- **Websites & Apps:** User-friendly interfaces translate your actions (clicking a button, filling a form) into the corresponding API calls.
- **Libraries & Tools:** Developers use specialized tools and libraries that handle communication with various APIs, simplifying the integration process.

A Note on API Documentation

For developers and businesses looking to utilize specific APIs, good documentation is key! Clear API documentation explains its purpose, how to make requests, and the expected data structures.

Additional Resources

- **Exploring Public APIs:** Directories like ProgrammableWeb can help you discover interesting APIs to experiment with: https://www.programmableweb.com/apis/directory
- **"How APIs Work (for Non-Developers)"** An article offering a conceptual overview: https://www.mulesoft.com/resources/api/what-is-an-api

Next Up: Understanding the Conversation Between Requests and Responses

APIs facilitate a constant conversation between applications. Let's dive into how requests and responses work together and decipher the language they speak.

Dialogue Between Requests and Responses

Just like any conversation, there's a back-and-forth between the system making an API request (the client) and the server responding to it. Understanding this dialogue is key to grasping how APIs enable data flow.

The Request: Setting the Stage

An API request is carefully composed with several essential elements:

- **HTTP Method:** GET, POST, PUT, DELETE, etc., tell the server what action is intended.
- **URL:** The address of the resource the client wants to interact with.
- **Headers:** Optional, they carry metadata like authentication tokens or information about the data format.
- **Body:** Sometimes included (like with POST or PUT requests) to send new data to the server.

The Response: The Server's Answer

Once the server processes the request, it sends back an API response:

- **Status Code** This special code signals the overall outcome (more on this in the next chapter!) Examples: "200 OK" for success, "404 Not Found," etc.
- **Headers:** The response also includes headers with metadata like the content type (JSON, etc.)
- **Body:** Usually present, containing the data requested by the client (if successful) or an error message describing a problem.

Real World Analogy

Here's a simplified way to think about requests and responses:

- **You (the client):** Order a cappuccino at a coffee shop.
- **Request:** "One cappuccino, extra hot, to-go."
- **Server (the barista):** Processes your order.
- **Response:** * **Status:** Either your cappuccino is ready or a message explaining why it can't be made. * **Body:** The cappuccino itself (if successful).

Example: Let's see a simplified GET request and response:

Request

GET https://api.weatherapp.com/forecast?city=Tokyo

Possible Response

Status Code: 200 OK

Content-Type: application/json

{

  "city": "Tokyo",

  "current_temp": 18,

  "conditions": "Partly Cloudy"

}

The Power of Conversation

This request-response exchange is the foundation upon which complex functionality is built:

- **Chained Requests:** One API response might provide data that triggers another request.
- **Real-time Interaction:** APIs facilitate responsive websites that can be updated with fresh data without a full page reload.

Additional Resources

- **Learn about HTTP: The protocol behind API communication:** https://developer.mozilla.org/en-US/docs/Web/HTTP
- **HTTP Viewer Tools:** See API requests and responses in action! Try a browser extension like "RESTED" or use the Network tab in your browser's developer tools.

Next: Cracking the Code of Status Codes!

Status codes, those little numbers in API responses, hold vital clues about the success or failure of your requests. Let's learn to decipher their language!

Deciphering the Language of Status Codes

Think of status codes as the API server's way of giving you a short report card after each request. They might seem cryptic at first, but learning to interpret them is crucial for both users and developers who interact with APIs.

Status Code Categories

Status codes fall into distinct ranges, each with a broad meaning:

- **1xx (Informational):** Rarely seen by regular users. Indicates the request is still being processed.
- **2xx (Success):** Yahoo! Your request went through! The most common example is "200 OK."
- **3xx (Redirection):** The resource might have moved; the server tells you where to look next.
- **4xx (Client Error):** Oops, you likely made a mistake. Examples are "404 Not Found" or "400 Bad Request" (something wrong with the request itself).
- **5xx (Server Error):** Uh-oh! Something went wrong on the server's end, and it couldn't fulfill your request.

Common Status Codes You Might Encounter

- **200 OK:** All good! The standard for successful GET, PUT, or PATCH requests.
- **201 Created:** Success when a POST request results in a new resource being created.
- **400 Bad Request:** Something's not right with your request's format (incorrect data, etc.).
- **401 Unauthorized:** You need to provide login credentials to access this resource.
- **403 Forbidden:** You're authenticated, but don't have permission to do that.
- **404 Not Found:** The resource you asked for doesn't exist.
- **500 Internal Server Error:** A general catch-all for server-side problems.

Why Status Codes Matter

- **For Users:** While apps often shield you from the raw codes, understanding the basics will improve your troubleshooting when things don't work (e.g., a 404 lets you know to check your URL for a typo).
- **For Developers:** Status codes are essential when building applications that use APIs. You need to handle different responses gracefully to provide a good user experience.

Example: Submitting a Signup Form

- **Scenario: Success**
    - Status Code: 201 Created
- **Scenario: Email Already Exists**
    - Status Code: 400 Bad Request (with a clear error message in the response)
- **Scenario: Internal Database Problem**
    - Status Code: 500 Internal Server Error

Helpful Tools

Status codes can get very specific! Here are resources to help you look them up:

- **MDN Web Docs – HTTP Status Codes:** https://developer.mozilla.org/en-US/docs/Web/HTTP/Status
- **HTTP Status Code List:** https://httpstatuses.com/

Additional Resources

- **"Making Sense of HTTP Status Codes" Article:** https://developer.mozilla.org/en-US/docs/Web/HTTP/Status

Next Up: Keeping Your APIs Safe

With a grasp on how APIs communicate, it's time to explore API security. How do we ensure that sensitive data remains protected in our API-driven world?

Safeguarding Your APIs: The Realm of API Security

APIs are like gateways in the digital realm, enabling data to flow in both directions. Unfortunately, this also makes them potential targets for malicious actors. A poorly secured API can have serious consequences:

- **Data Breaches:** Sensitive information like customer data, financial details, or trade secrets could be exposed.
- **Unauthorized Access:** Attackers could gain control of user accounts or tamper with resources within the system connected to the API.
- **Disruption of Service:** APIs can be bombarded with requests (sometimes called a Denial of Service attack), making the service unusable for legitimate users.

Security Needs a Multifaceted Approach

Ensuring API security isn't a one-time fix. It requires a combination of strategies:

- **Authentication:** The cornerstone! Verify the identity of the user or application making the API calls. This often involves API keys, tokens, or more complex systems like OAuth.
- **Authorization:** Even if a user is known, determine what they're allowed to do. Restrict access to resources and actions based on carefully defined permissions.
- **Input Validation:** Never trust data coming from the outside. Check all input to make sure it's in the expected format and sanitize it to prevent attacks like SQL injection.
- **Rate Limiting:** Protect against excessive requests that could overload your system, whether accidental or malicious.
- **Encryption:** Secure data in transit using HTTPS to prevent snooping. For sensitive data, consider encryption at rest as well.
- **Regular Monitoring and Auditing:** Keep a close eye on your API logs to detect any suspicious activity or unusual usage patterns.

A User's Perspective on API Security

While your primary interaction with security might be entering passwords or receiving verification codes, here's what you should look for as an API user:

- **Use Well-Established APIs:** Choose APIs from reputable providers with a track record of good security practices.
- **HTTPS is a Must:** Ensure the API endpoints you're using are secured with HTTPS (look for the padlock in your browser).
- **Be Cautious with Permissions:** When granting an app or service access to an API on your behalf, carefully review which permissions are being requested.

Security for Developers

If you're building applications using APIs, security needs to be front-and-center in your design:

- **Best Practices:** Follow industry-standard best practices for API security. There are excellent resources available from organizations like OWASP.
- **Vulnerability Testing:** Regularly test your APIs for known weaknesses and fix any potential issues you uncover.
- **Minimize Data Exposure:** Limit the amount of sensitive information accessible even to authorized users.

Additional Resources

- **OWASP API Security Project:** https://owasp.org/www-project-api-security/
- **API Security Checklist:** https://github.com/shieldfy/API-Security-Checklist

API Security is an Ongoing Journey

The threat landscape is constantly evolving, so API security needs to be an ongoing concern. Stay informed, prioritize security, and protect the valuable data and functions your APIs provide.

Next Section: Mastering API Integration

Now that you have a foundation in core API concepts, let's transition into the next section. Here, we'll focus on the practical skills for integrating APIs into applications or workflows, including topics like documentation, versioning, and more!

Section 3:
Mastering API Integration

Best Practices for API Documentation: Crafting Clear Guidelines

Great API documentation isn't just about explaining technical details; it's about enabling users to succeed. Whether you're documenting your own API or need to evaluate someone else's, this chapter will cover the essential elements.

Why API Documentation is Crucial

- **Onboarding New Users:** Clear documentation makes it easy for developers to start using your API quickly, increasing the chances of adoption.
- **Long-Term Reference:** Even experienced users need a reference to refresh their memory on specifics of the API usage.
- **Minimizing Support Requests:** Well-written documentation answers common questions, reducing the need for direct assistance.
- **Promoting Consistency:** Documentation encourages best practices and prevents incorrect implementation.

Key Components of Excellent API Documentation

1. **Getting Started Guide:**
    - A quick-start tutorial to get a basic request and response working. A "Hello World" for your API!
    - Cover installation of required libraries or tools, and setup (like obtaining API keys).
2. **Authentication and Authorization:**
    - Clearly explain the authentication mechanism (API keys, OAuth, etc.).
    - Specify required permissions/scopes for accessing different resources.
3. **Resource Descriptions and Endpoints:**

- List available resources and their associated URLs.
- Detail the supported HTTP methods (GET, POST, etc.) for each one.
4. **Parameters and Query Options:**
    - Describe all accepted parameters (required and optional) with data types.
    - Explain filtering, sorting, or pagination features.
5. **Request and Response Examples:**
    - Include **for each endpoint** examples of valid requests and their corresponding responses (including the format, like JSON).
6. **Error Codes and Handling:**
    - List possible status codes, what they mean, and guidance on troubleshooting.
7. **Rate Limits and Usage Quotas:**
    - Be upfront about any restrictions to manage requests and prevent abuse.

Beyond the Basics

- **Interactive Documentation:** Tools like Swagger UI allow users to try out API requests directly within the documentation – making it super user-friendly.
- **Sample Code:** Providing snippets in different programming languages lowers the barrier to entry.
- **SDKs:** Client libraries make integration even easier for developers.

Good Documentation is an Investment

Treat your API documentation with as much care as the API itself. It directly impacts:

- **Developer Experience:** Smooth experience leads to happier users and wider adoption of your API.
- **Maintainability:** Good documentation makes it easier to update your API with less risk of breaking things for existing users.

Additional Resources

- **"Write the Docs" Community:** https://www.writethedocs.org/
- **API Documentation Tools:** https://swagger.io/tools/open-source/open-source-integrations/

Next Up: Managing Changes with API Versioning

APIs evolve over time. Let's explore how versioning allows for updates and improvements without breaking existing applications that rely on your API.

Versioning APIs: Managing Changes Seamlessly

Imagine an API as a contract between a provider (the server) and its consumers (the apps using it). Versioning is like having a system for revising that contract while ensuring things still work for those who agreed to previous versions.

Why Versioning Matters

- **Backwards Compatibility:** If you change an API in a way that breaks existing apps reliant on the old format or behavior, you'll create unhappy users. Versioning helps avoid this.
- **Controlled Evolution:** You should be able to add new features or restructure an API without forcing everyone to update immediately.
- **Deprecation:** Versioning provides a way to gracefully phase out old API versions, giving users time to migrate.

Common Versioning Schemes

1. **In the URL:** One of the simplest methods. Embed the version number directly into the API endpoint URLs.
    - Example:
        - `https://api.example.com/v1/products`
        - `https://api.example.com/v2/products`
2. **HTTP Headers:** A more subtle approach using custom headers.
    - Example: Clients might include a header like `Accept: application/vnd.example.v2+json`.
3. **Query Parameter:** Less common, but possible.
    - Example: `https://api.example.com/products?version=2`

Choosing a Strategy

- **URL Versioning:** Often preferred due to clarity and ease of implementation.
- **Header-Based:** Might be best if you want to keep URLs cleaner, but there's a little more setup required for the client.

Communicating Version Changes

Clear documentation is crucial when managing multiple API versions. Highlight:

- **Changelog:** A detailed list of changes introduced in each version.
- **Deprecation Timeline:** Announce when old versions will be sunsetted, giving users ample time to update.

Example: Versioning a Weather API

- **Original:** `/weather?city=London`
- **New Version (v2):** `/v2/weather?city=London&units=metric` (adds the option for metric units)

For Users of APIs

- **Look for Versioning:** Is it in the URL? Are custom headers required? This information should be in the API documentation.
- **Stay Updated:** Check for change announcements to avoid surprises when old versions are retired.

Additional Resources

- **API Versioning Guide:** https://www.smashingmagazine.com/2018/01/moving-from-react-redux-graphql/
- **"How to Design a Good API and Why it Matters" Article** https://www.howtogeek.com/343877/how-to-design-a-good-api-and-why-it-matters/

Next: Making Your API Speedy!

Now that you understand how to manage API updates gracefully, let's turn our focus to performance optimization, ensuring your API can handle requests swiftly and efficiently.

Performance Optimization Techniques: Maximizing Efficiency

Picture your API as a busy highway. The goal of optimization is to increase the number of cars (requests) that can travel smoothly without causing any traffic jams (bottlenecks).

Why Performance is Paramount

- **User Experience:** Slow loading times lead to frustration and abandonment. Snappy APIs are essential for keeping users engaged.
- **Scalability:** An inefficient API will buckle under the pressure of increased traffic. Optimizations make your API ready for growth.
- **Resource Costs:** Poorly designed APIs can consume excessive resources (server power, database queries), driving up your operating costs.

Where to Look for Bottlenecks

- **Network Latency:** The physical distance between the client and server can introduce delays.
- **Slow Database Queries:** Inefficient database operations can significantly slow down response times.
- **Unnecessary Computations:** Is your API doing more work than needed? Complex calculations can take a toll.
- **External Dependencies:** If your API relies on third-party services, their speed will affect yours.

Optimization Strategies

1. **Caching:** The star player! Store frequently requested data in a temporary location (like in-memory caches or Content Delivery Networks (CDNs)) for faster retrieval.
2. **Database Optimization:** Ensure your database is indexed properly and queries are written efficiently.
3. **Efficient Code:** Avoid redundant operations or heavy processes within your API's codebase.
4. **Compression:** Compress responses, especially large ones, using technologies like GZIP to reduce data transfer time.
5. **Pagination:** Break down large result sets into smaller pages. This improves response times, especially for resource lists.

6. **Load Balancing**: If your API receives a surge of traffic, distribute the load across multiple servers to prevent overload.

Developer Considerations

- **Be Mindful of Client-side Requests:** Design your frontend to avoid making an excessive number of API calls.
- **Choose the Right Tools:** Use specialized tools for load testing your API, identifying potential areas for improvement.

Additional Resources

- **Web.dev Articles on Performance:** https://web.dev/learn/ (Search for performance-related topics)
- **API Performance Checklist:** https://blog.postman.com/api-performance-testing/

Monitoring: Continuous Improvement

Optimization isn't a one-time thing! Regular monitoring of your API's performance will help you identify and fix emerging issues before they severely impact your users.

Next: Proactive Error Handling in APIs

Even the best-performing APIs can encounter problems. Let's discuss how to gracefully handle errors and communicate them effectively to your API users.

Error Handling Strategies: Navigating Through Challenges

Imagine error handling as providing a helpful roadmap when your API journey takes an unexpected detour. A well-designed error handling approach is crucial for a positive user experience, especially for developers.

Why Error Handling is Essential

- **User Frustration:** Vague errors leave users confused and irritated. Clear messages empower them to resolve issues.
- **Debugging:** Detailed error messages help developers pinpoint the root cause of problems, speeding up bug fixing.
- **Robustness:** A well-defined error handling strategy makes your API more resilient in the face of unexpected problems.

The Anatomy of an API Error Response

While there's some flexibility, good error responses should include:

- **HTTP Status Code:** The appropriate code from the 400s (client-side error) or 500s (server-side error). We covered these in Chapter 15!
- **Error Code:** A machine-readable, unique code that helps classify the type of error (e.g., "INVALID_PARAMETER", "RESOURCE_NOT_FOUND").
- **Error Message:** A human-readable, concise description of the problem. Try to avoid overly technical jargon.

Example: Error Response

```
{
  "statusCode": 400,
  "errorCode": "MISSING_REQUIRED_FIELD",
  "message": "Field 'email' is required."
}
```

Types of Errors

- **Client Errors (4xx):** The user probably needs to fix something in their request (incorrect data, missing authorization, etc.).

- **Server Errors (5xx):** An issue on your end occurred (database down, internal bug, etc.).
- **Rate Limiting Errors:** A specific status code (usually 429 - Too Many Requests) to indicate a user needs to slow down.

Pointers for Developers

- **Be Specific:** Generic messages aren't helpful. Give developers enough information to act.
- **Don't Overexpose:** Avoid leaking sensitive internal implementation details in your errors.
- **Error Documentation:** Include in your API documentation a full list of possible error codes and their explanations.

From a User's Perspective

Even without coding, you can learn to decode simple errors:

- **400s:** Check your request format, look for missing or incorrect fields.
- **401/403:** An issue with your authentication credentials or permissions.
- **500s:** Likely a temporary server-side issue. May require contacting support.

Additional Resources

- **How to Design Better API Error Responses:** https://www.freecodecamp.org/news/restful-api-design-how-to-design-better-error-handling-responses/
- **REST API Error Codes Best Practices:** https://www.restapitutorial.com/httpstatuscodes.html

Next: Ensuring API Reliability with Testing

Error handling is reactive – dealing with problems that already occurred. But what about preventing them? In the next chapter, we'll delve into API testing!

API Testing Essentials: Ensuring Reliability

Building an API is only half the battle. Rigorous testing is essential to verify it behaves correctly, delivers expected results, and handles unexpected situations gracefully.

Why API Testing Is Critical

- **Catch Bugs Early:** Finding errors before your API is used in production saves a lot of headaches and potential problems down the line.
- **Confidence in Changes:** As you evolve your API, tests provide a safety net, ensuring new features don't break existing functionality.
- **Maintainability:** A well-tested API is easier to update with reduced fear of unintended consequences.
- **User Trust:** Thorough testing translates into a reliable service, fostering confidence in users of your API.

Types of API Tests

Let's look at some common categories:

- **Functional Tests:** The core of API testing. These verify if the API outputs match the expected results for various input scenarios.
- **Performance/Load Tests:** Subject your API to simulated heavy usage. How does it hold up under pressure?
- **Security Tests:** Probe for vulnerabilities like unauthorized access or susceptibility to injection attacks.
- **Integration Tests:** Ensure your API functions smoothly when working with other systems it relies on.

Test Scenarios to Focus On

- **Valid Inputs:** Cover a range of typical and edge-case scenarios for data your API should accept.
- **Invalid Inputs:** How does the API handle incorrect data, missing fields, or unexpected formats?
- **Negative Tests:** Ensure the correct error responses are generated as per your error handling strategy.
- **Authentication and Authorization:** Test various permission levels and try unauthorized requests.

Tools of the Trade

While you won't be writing test code, understanding some tools is helpful:

- **API Testing Frameworks:** Specialized tools like Postman, REST Assured, and Karate provide structure and features for creating and managing tests.
- **Load Testing Tools:** JMeter and Locust help simulate heavy API traffic.

API Testing for Developers

- **Test-Driven Development (TDD):** Write tests *before* developing the code. This forces you to think about how your API should function.
- **Continuous Integration:** Automate running tests after every code change to catch regressions quickly.

Additional Resources

- "API Testing Basics" Article: https://www.guru99.com/api-testing.html
- API Testing Tools: https://www.softwaretestinghelp.com/api-testing-tools/

The Importance of Monitoring and Analytics

Testing doesn't end with deployment! The next chapter will focus on monitoring your API in production to ensure continued health and performance.

Monitoring and Analytics: Keeping a Pulse on Your APIs

Think of monitoring and analytics as having a stethoscope for your API. They enable you to detect issues early, track usage patterns, and gain insights to make informed decisions about its improvement.

Why Monitoring and Analytics Matter

- **Proactive Troubleshooting:** Be alerted to errors or performance dips before they severely impact your users.
- **Capacity Planning:** Understand your API's usage trends, ensuring you have enough resources to handle demand.
- **Business Insights:** Are certain parts of your API used more than others? Analytics can influence future development.
- **Detect Abuse:** Identify abnormal usage patterns that might signal misuse of your API.

Key Metrics to Monitor

- **Response Times:** How quickly does your API respond to requests? Watch for slowdowns or spikes.
- **Error Rates:** Track any 4xx or 5xx status codes, drilling down into specific error types for troubleshooting.
- **Traffic Volume:** The number of requests your API gets over time
- **Uptime/Availability:** Is your API consistently reachable?
- **API Usage by Resource:** Monitor which endpoints get the most and least traffic.

How Analytics Adds Value

Let's look at some questions analytics can answer:

- **Who is Using Your API?** Insights into user demographics or integration with partner systems.
- **Most Popular Endpoints:** Helps direct development focus on the most essential areas of your API.
- **Performance over Time:** Identify any long-term performance trends or degradation.

Tools and Techniques

- **Logging:** The foundation! Ensure your API logs requests, response times, errors, and any relevant data.
- **Monitoring Dashboards:** Tools to visualize key metrics, providing an at-a-glance overview of API health.
- **Alerting Systems:** Get notifications when thresholds are exceeded (e.g., high error rates, API goes down).
- **Analytics Platforms:** Specialized tools for deeper analysis of usage trends and behavior patterns.

User-Focused Insights

While monitoring is often technical, analytics can directly benefit API consumers:

- **Status Page:** A public page transparently showing your API's current uptime and historical incidents.
- **Usage Statistics:** For developers using your API, providing insights into their own API call patterns can be valuable.

Additional Resources

- **API Monitoring Best Practices:** https://www.dynatrace.com/news/blog/api-monitoring-best-practices/
- **API Analytics Tools:** https://apimetrics.io/api-analytics-tools/

Next Up: Planning for API Growth

Your API won't stay small forever (hopefully!). Let's discuss strategies in the next chapter to ensure your API scales gracefully to meet increasing demand.

Scalability Considerations: Preparing for Growth

Think of scalability as the ability of your API to gracefully adjust to fluctuations in demand. Designing with scalability in mind from the start can make a huge difference for the long-term success of your API.

Factors Affecting Scalability

- **Traffic Volume:** Can your API handle sudden spikes in requests?
- **Data Size:** As your API's database or storage needs grow, how will you adapt?
- **Complexity of Operations:** Computationally heavy requests might require specialized scaling strategies.

Key Scalability Strategies

1. **Load Balancing:** Distribute incoming requests across multiple servers rather than overloading a single one. Prevents bottlenecks.
2. **Caching (We Revisited!)** Store frequently requested data in memory or CDNs to reduce database strain and serve responses faster.
3. **Optimize Database**: Proper indexing, efficient queries, and sometimes the choice of database technology itself (e.g., scaling out a relational database vs. using a document-oriented one designed for high volumes).
4. **Asynchronous Operations:** Break down long-running tasks into smaller chunks that can be processed in the background without holding up user requests.
5. **Serverless Architecture:** For APIs with unpredictable traffic patterns, serverless platforms (like AWS Lambda) can automatically scale up and down as needed.

When Scaling Becomes Complex

- **Microservices:** Break up a large API into smaller, independently scalable services. This can offer more granular control.
- **Horizontal vs. Vertical Scaling:** Adding more servers (horizontal) vs. upgrading existing hardware (vertical). Your choice depends on your API's nature.

Scalability for Users and Developers

- **Clear Rate Limits:** Be transparent about usage quotas and provide clear instructions for increasing limits when needed.
- **Prepare for Version Changes:** As you scale, your API might evolve. Chapter 18 (on versioning) is crucial here!

Additional Resources

- **API Scalability Best Practices:**
  https://nordicapis.com/api-scalability-best-practices/
- **"Architecting for Scale" (AWS Whitepaper):** Offers general scalability principles, though examples are AWS-specific:
  https://d1.awsstatic.com/whitepapers/AWS_Cloud_Best_Practices.pdf

Scalability and Monitoring Go Hand in Hand

The metrics you monitor (Chapter 22) will be your early warning system for when it's time to scale your API infrastructure.

Let's Talk About the Future!

In the final chapter, we'll take a peek into emerging trends and innovations shaping the future of APIs and web communication.

Future Trends in Web Communication: Embracing Innovations

The world of APIs is constantly evolving. Here's a glimpse at some of the directions in which it's heading:

Trend 1: The Rise of GraphQL

- **Beyond REST:** GraphQL offers an alternative to RESTful APIs. Clients can request *exactly* the data they need in a single query, reducing over-fetching and multiple roundtrips.
- **Flexibility for Frontends:** Especially powerful for applications with dynamic data requirements.

Trend 2: Real-Time APIs

- **Instant Updates:** WebSockets and other technologies allow APIs to "push" updates to clients instead of only responding to requests.
- **Use Cases:** Chat systems, live dashboards, stock tickers, collaborative tools thrive on real-time communication.

Trend 3: APIs in the Internet of Things (IoT)

- **Connected World:** APIs enable the flow of data and control commands between countless smart devices, buildings, cars, and more.
- **Standardization Challenges:** With diverse IoT devices and protocols, establishing common API standards remains a work in progress.

Trend 4: Low-Code / No-Code API Building

- **Democratization of API Development:** Visual tools allow users to create APIs without extensive programming knowledge.
- **Empowers Non-Technical Users:** Opens doors for businesses and individuals to harness the potential of APIs without a large development team.

Trend 5: AI-Powered APIs

- **APIs Get Smarter:** Expect APIs that offer language processing, image recognition, and other AI-enabled capabilities.
- **New Possibilities:** This expands the scope of what APIs can do, fueling creative innovation

The Growing Importance of API Ecosystems

- **Beyond Individual APIs:** We're increasingly seeing platforms and marketplaces where numerous APIs are aggregated and work together.
- **Focus on Discoverability:** Finding the right APIs and integrating them seamlessly will become even more crucial.

Additional Resources

- **GraphQL Website:** https://graphql.org/
- **WebSockets explained:** https://developer.mozilla.org/en-US/docs/Web/API/WebSockets_API

A Word of Caution: Continuous Learning

The landscape of web communication shifts rapidly. Being adaptable and staying curious are key for anyone using or building with APIs.

The Journey Continues!

I hope this book has empowered you with a solid understanding of the API world. Keep exploring, building, and contributing to the ever-connected future!

REST API Cheat Sheet

Here's a handy REST API Cheat Sheet, consolidating core concepts from our exploration of RESTful APIs. Designed to be a quick reference for those using and interacting with APIs!

REST Principles

- **Resources:** The building blocks. A resource could be a product, a customer, a blog post – anything of interest that the API is designed to work with.
- **Representations:** Resources can be represented in different formats (JSON being most common, but sometimes XML).
- **URLs:** Resources are identified by unique URLs (endpoints).
- **HTTP Methods:** Indicate the desired action on a resource: * **GET:** Read / retrieve data * **POST:** Create a new resource * **PUT:** Update an entire existing resource * **PATCH:** Modify a portion of an existing resource * **DELETE:** Remove a resource

HTTP Status Codes (Key Examples)

- **1xx:** Informational. Rarely encountered by end-users.
- **2xx Success:** * **200 OK:** General success * **201 Created:** After a successful POST request
- **3xx Redirection:** The client needs to take additional action for the request to complete.
- **4xx Client Error:** * **400 Bad Request:** Issue with the request format. * **401 Unauthorized:** Lack of authentication credentials. * **403 Forbidden:** User has credentials, but insufficient permissions. * **404 Not Found:** Resource wasn't found.
- **5xx Server Error:** * **500 Internal Server Error:** General server-side problem.

Common API Features

- **Authentication:** Mechanisms for verifying who's making the request (API keys, OAuth, etc.).
- **Authorization:** Determining what actions an authenticated user is allowed to perform.

- **Pagination:** Breaking down large datasets into smaller pages for easier retrieval.
- **Filtering and Sorting:** Options to refine API results.
- **Rate Limiting:** Setting limits on the number of requests to prevent abuse and overload.
- **Versioning:** Managing changes to an API with different versions indicated in the URL or headers.

Example: A Book API

Method	URL	Action
GET	`https://api.bookworld.com/books`	Fetches a list of available books
GET	`https://api.bookworld.com/books/1234`	Retrieves details of a book with ID 1234
POST	`https://api.bookworld.com/books`	Adds a new book to the catalog
PUT	`https://api.bookworld.com/books/1234`	Updates all details of the book with ID 1234
PATCH	`https://api.bookworld.com/books/1234`	Updates only specific fields (e.g., availability) of the book
DELETE	`https://api.bookworld.com/books/1234`	Deletes the book with ID 1234

Note: Specific URLs and methods can vary between APIs. Always consult the API's documentation for precise usage instructions.

Conclusion

APIs, our trusty digital bridges, have reshaped how we build software, interact online, and power our modern connected lives. Understanding the fundamentals behind them is more valuable than ever, whether you're a business owner, a tech enthusiast, or simply a curious user of the internet.

Let's recap some of the essentials you've discovered throughout this book:

- **APIs as a Language:** You've learned to speak the API language of requests and responses, URLs, HTTP methods, and status codes.
- **The Power of Data Exchange:** APIs enable the seamless flow of information that drives countless applications and experiences.
- **REST as a Guide:** RESTful principles provide a framework for designing predictable and easy-to-use APIs.
- **JSON Decoded:** You now see JSON as the go-to data format for most APIs, making data easily readable by both humans and machines.
- **API Superpowers in Your Hands:** From fetching weather information to automating tasks, you've seen how APIs unlock new possibilities.

API Skills for the Future

The world of APIs isn't static. Keeping an open mind and these core concepts close at hand will serve you well as you continue to interact with technology:

- **Embrace Learning:** Continuously update your understanding of new tools, trends, and best practices that shape the API landscape.
- **Think Like an API User:** When you encounter any website or app, consider the APIs that likely power its functionality under the surface.
- **Problem-Solver Mindset:** View APIs as tools to solve everyday problems or streamline workflows. Can an API help automate a task or integrate with other services you use?
- **Responsible Consumption:** Respect the limits and guidelines of APIs you use. Think about their creators and the resources powering them.

A Connected Journey Continues

The world of APIs is one of interconnection and boundless innovation. This book has served as your starting point. Now, go out there and explore! Search for interesting public APIs, read developer blogs, and don't be afraid to ask questions.

The best way to learn is by doing and observing. May your API adventures bring excitement and unlock new possibilities in your digital experiences!

Printed in Great Britain
by Amazon